College Coloring Books

Sisterhood Series

SIGMA SIGMA SIGMA

We love seeing completed work! Share your pics with us on social media or send via e-mail to gallery@collegecoloringbooks.com.

Request your custom coloring book today! Colleges, universities, sororities, fraternities, towns, and organizations can now request custom-designed adult coloring books for on- and off-campus bookstores, student/staff activities, admissions/recruiting, community and alumni fundraisers, and more. Special discounts are available on quantity purchases.

For permission requests, write to the publisher at the address below.

College Coloring Books

www.collegecoloringbooks.com   info@collegecoloringbooks.com   +1.571.424.1994

fb.me/CollegeColoringBooks   @collegecoloring   @college_coloring_books

ISBN-10: 1-945707-17-8   ISBN-13: 978-1-945707-17-9

Made in the USA

This book belongs to

of the

Chapter

of

Sigma Sigma Sigma

at

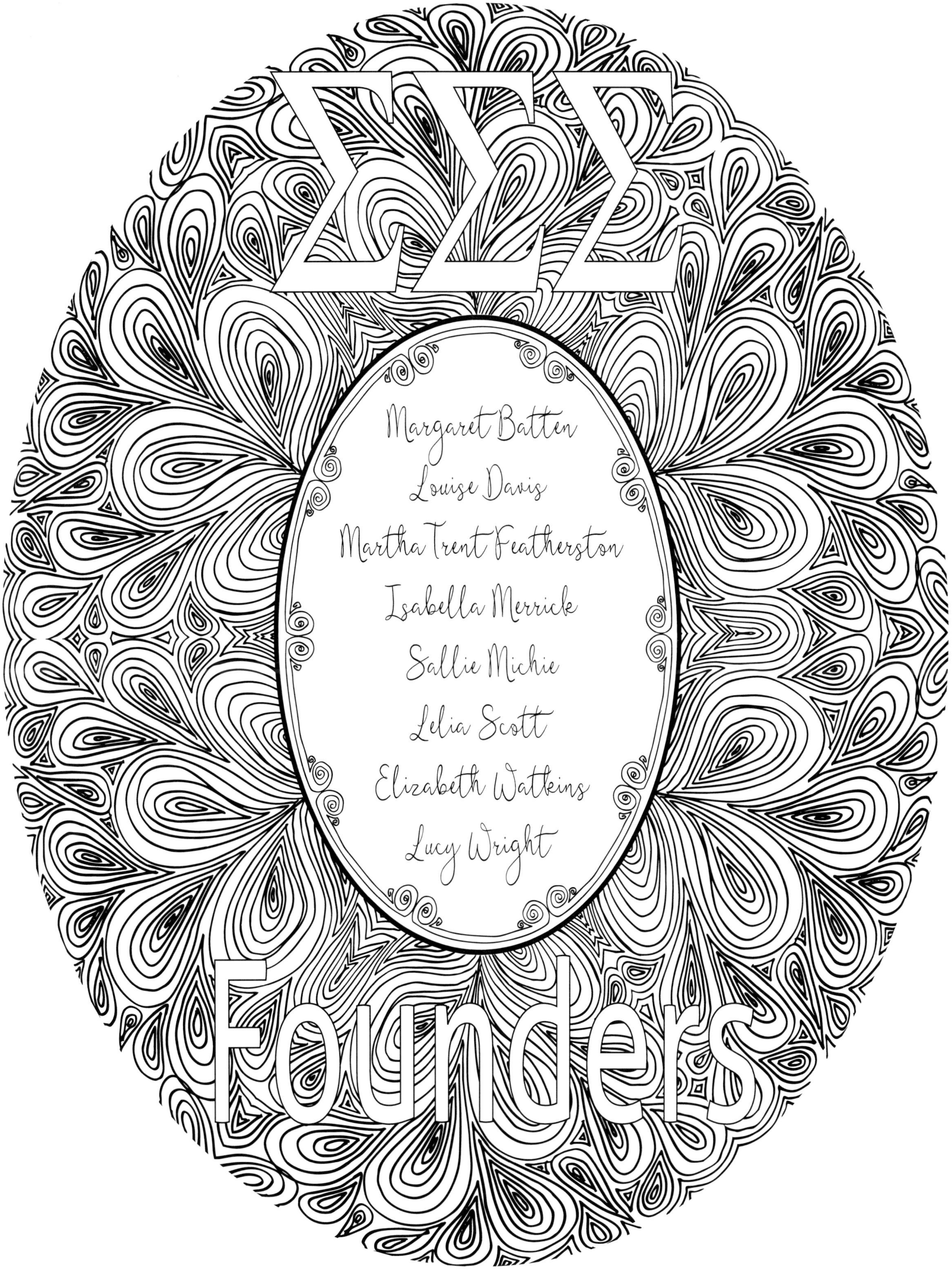
ΣΣΣ
Margaret Batten
Louise Davis
Martha Trent Featherston
Isabella Merrick
Sallie Michie
Lelia Scott
Elizabeth Watkins
Lucy Wright
Founders

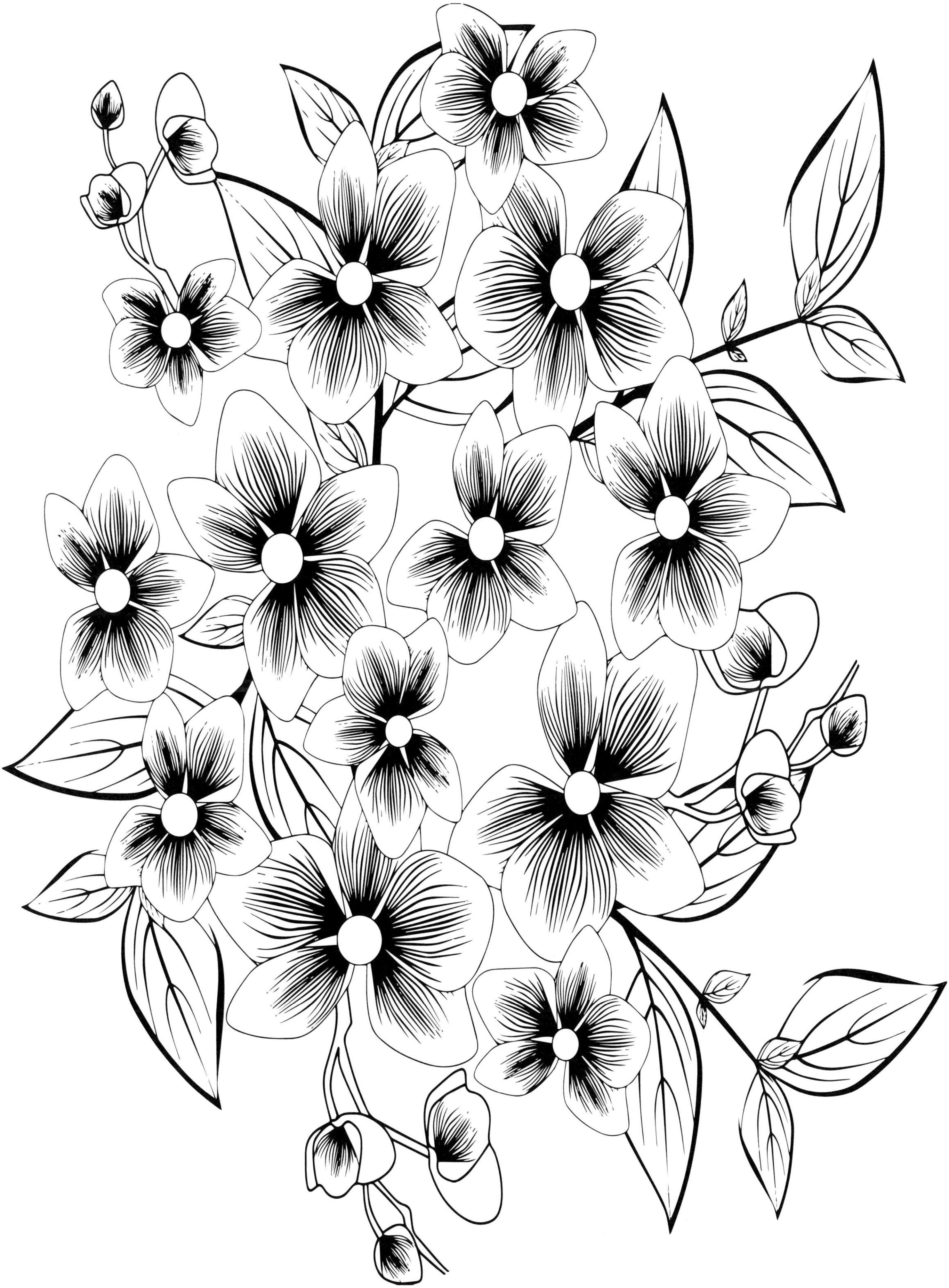

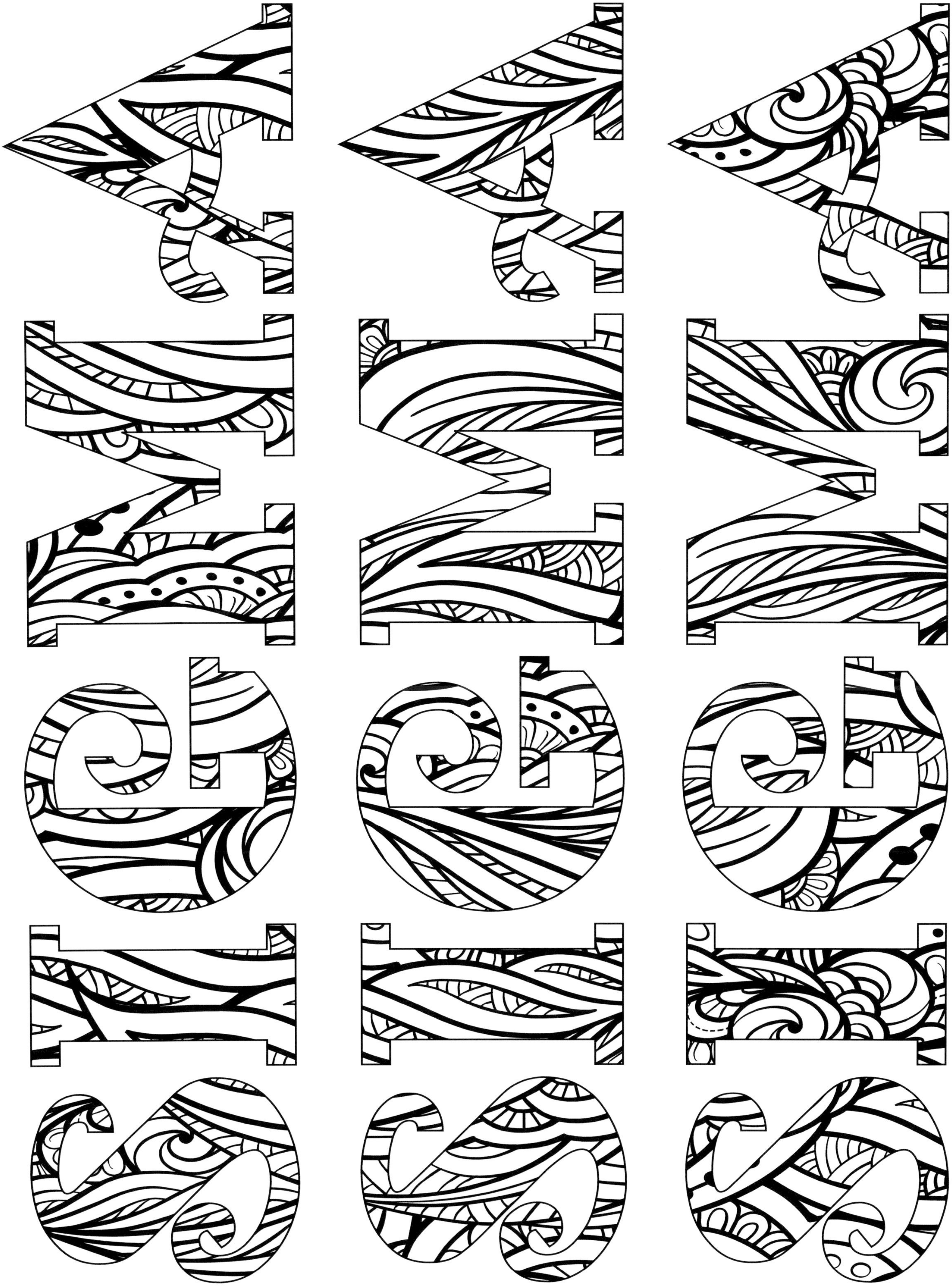

Side by side or miles apart,
we are sisters,
connected by the heart

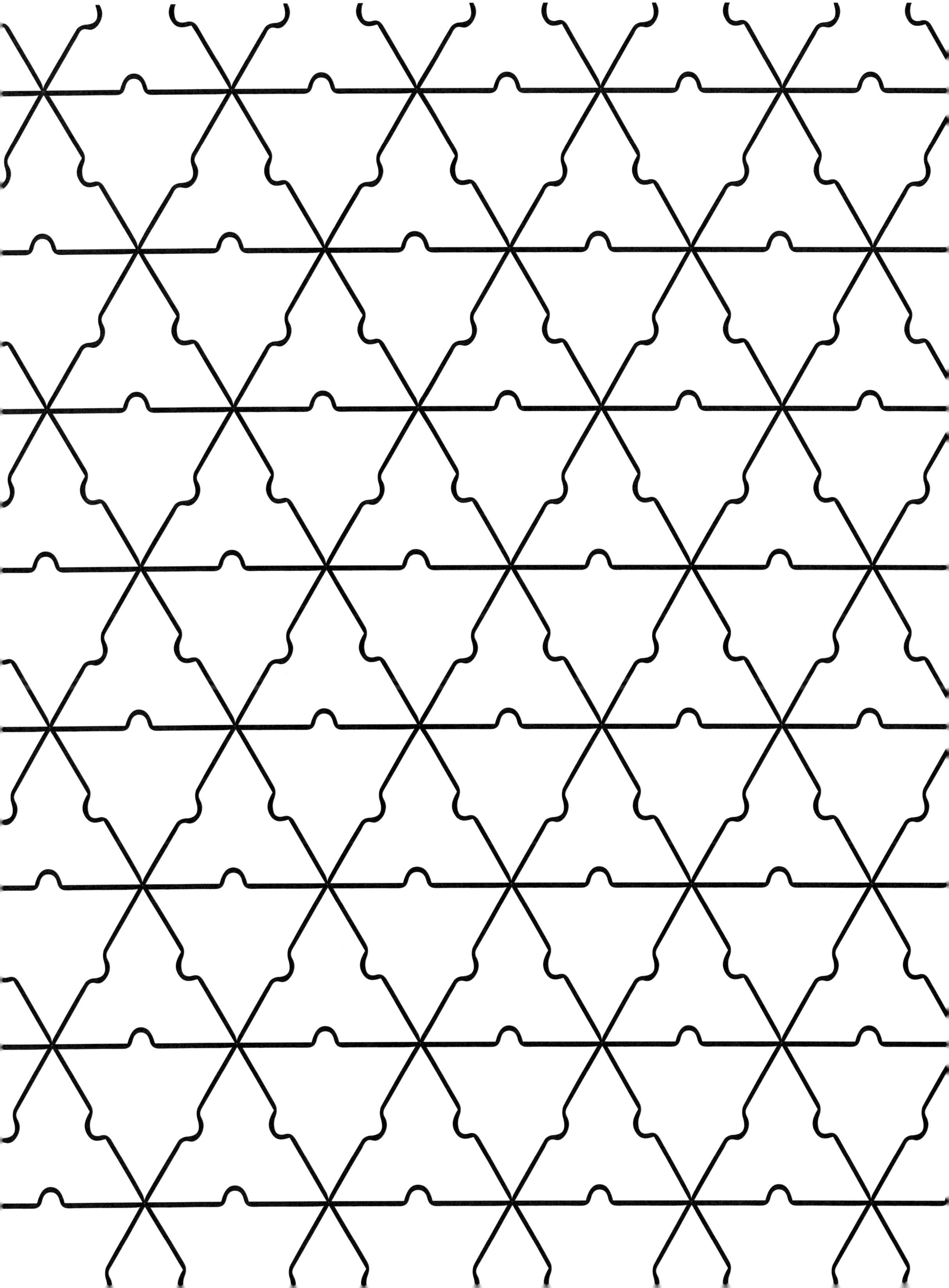

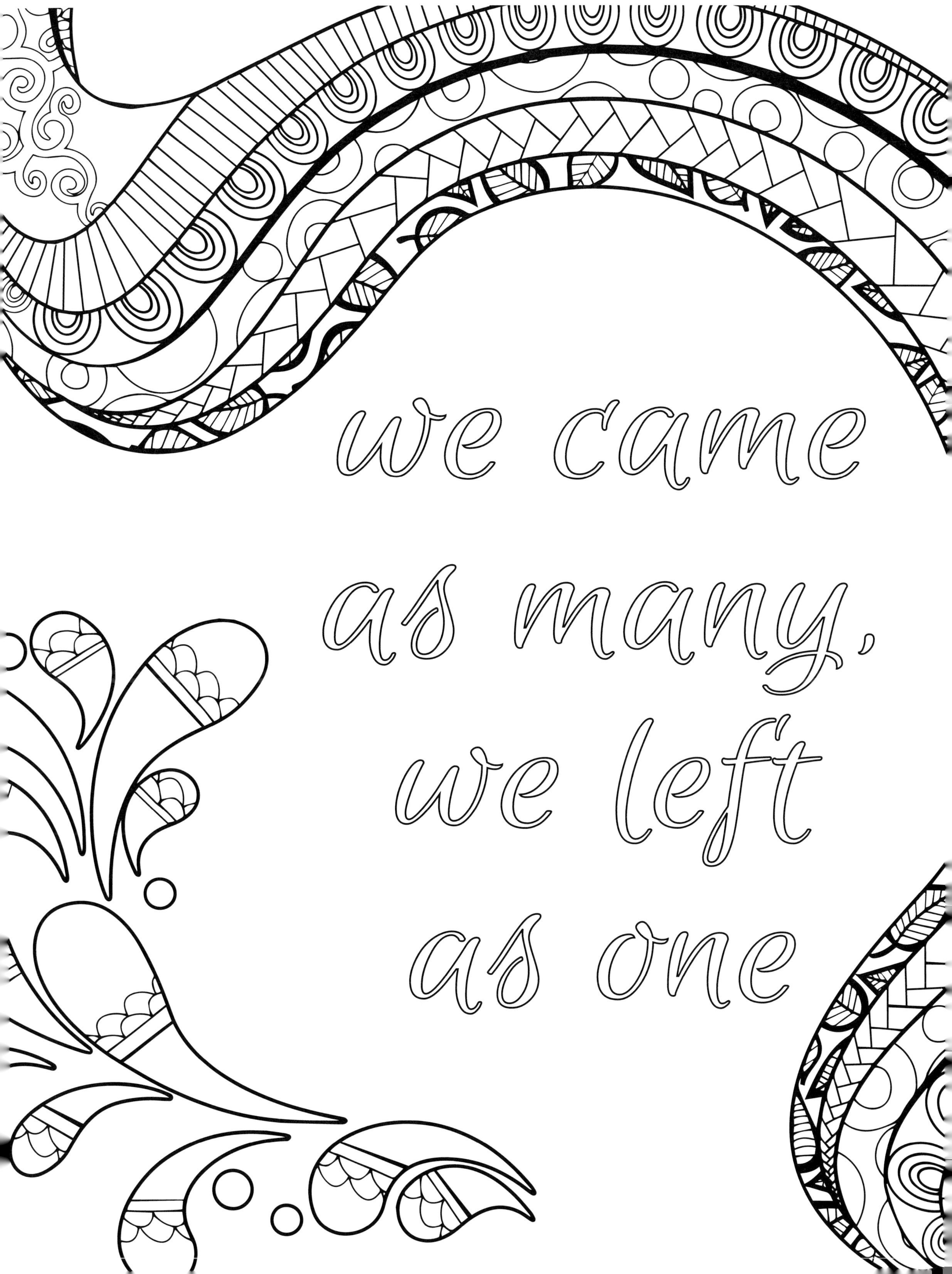
we came
as many,
we left
as one

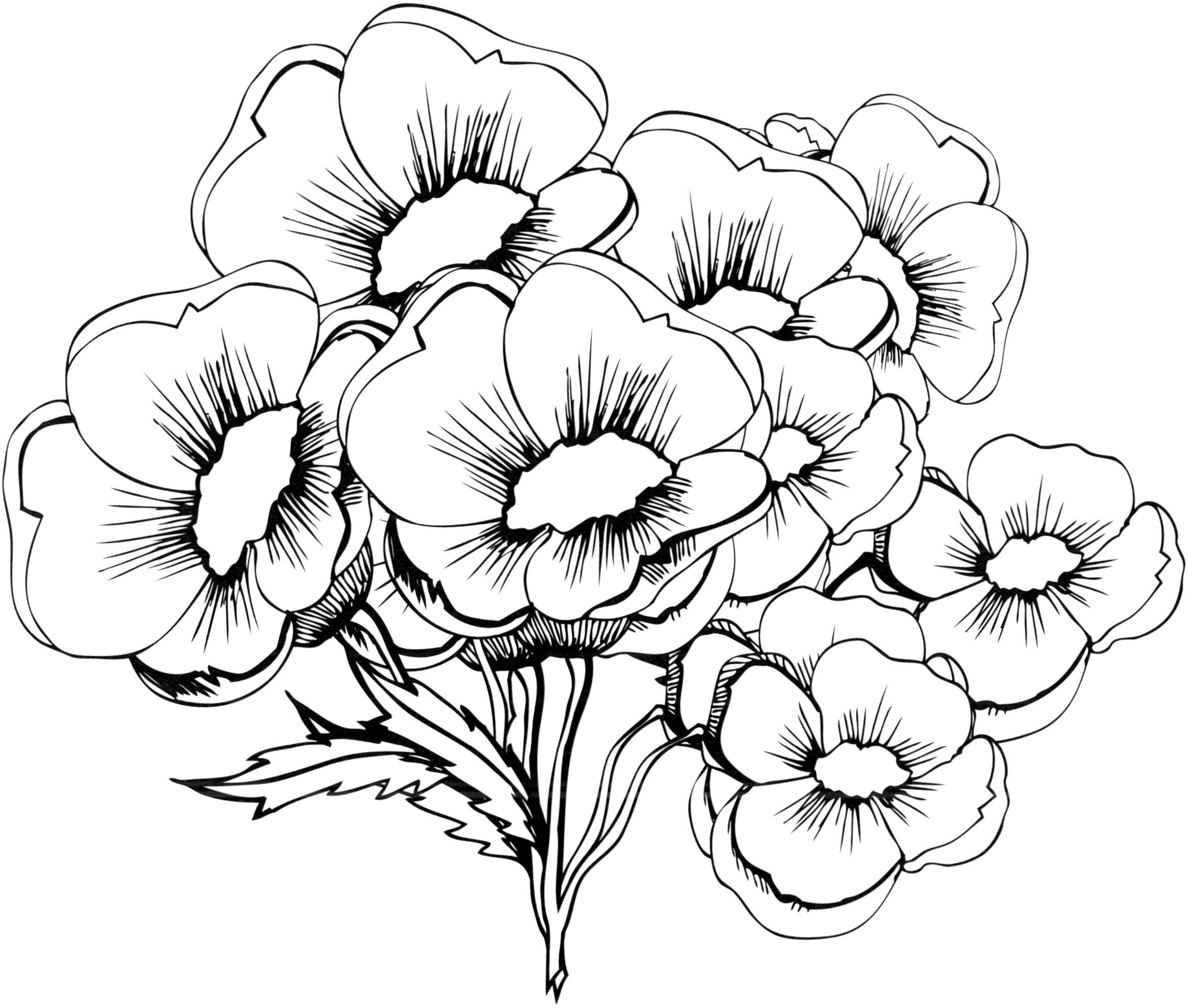

ΣΣΣ

Scholarship

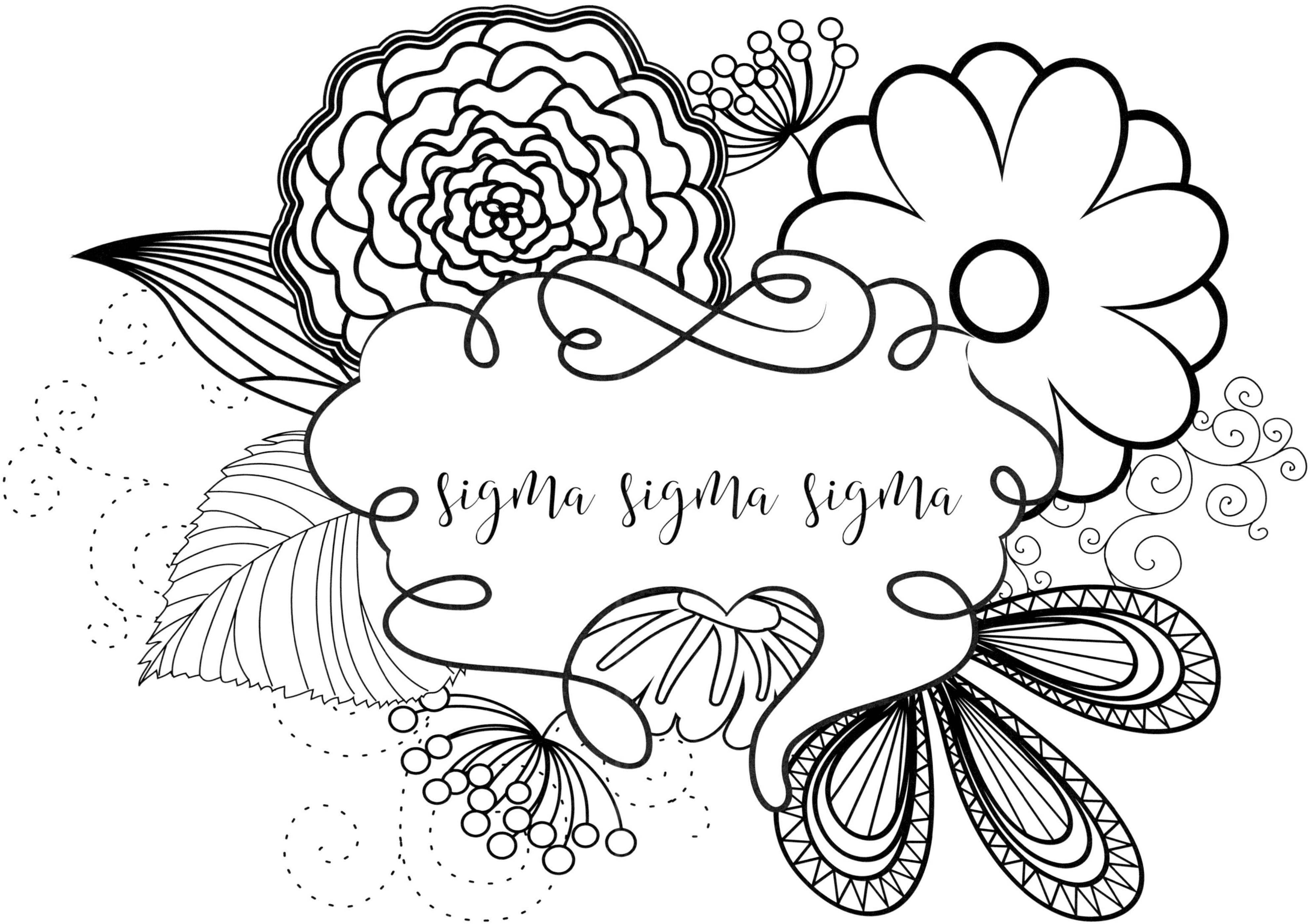
sigma sigma sigma

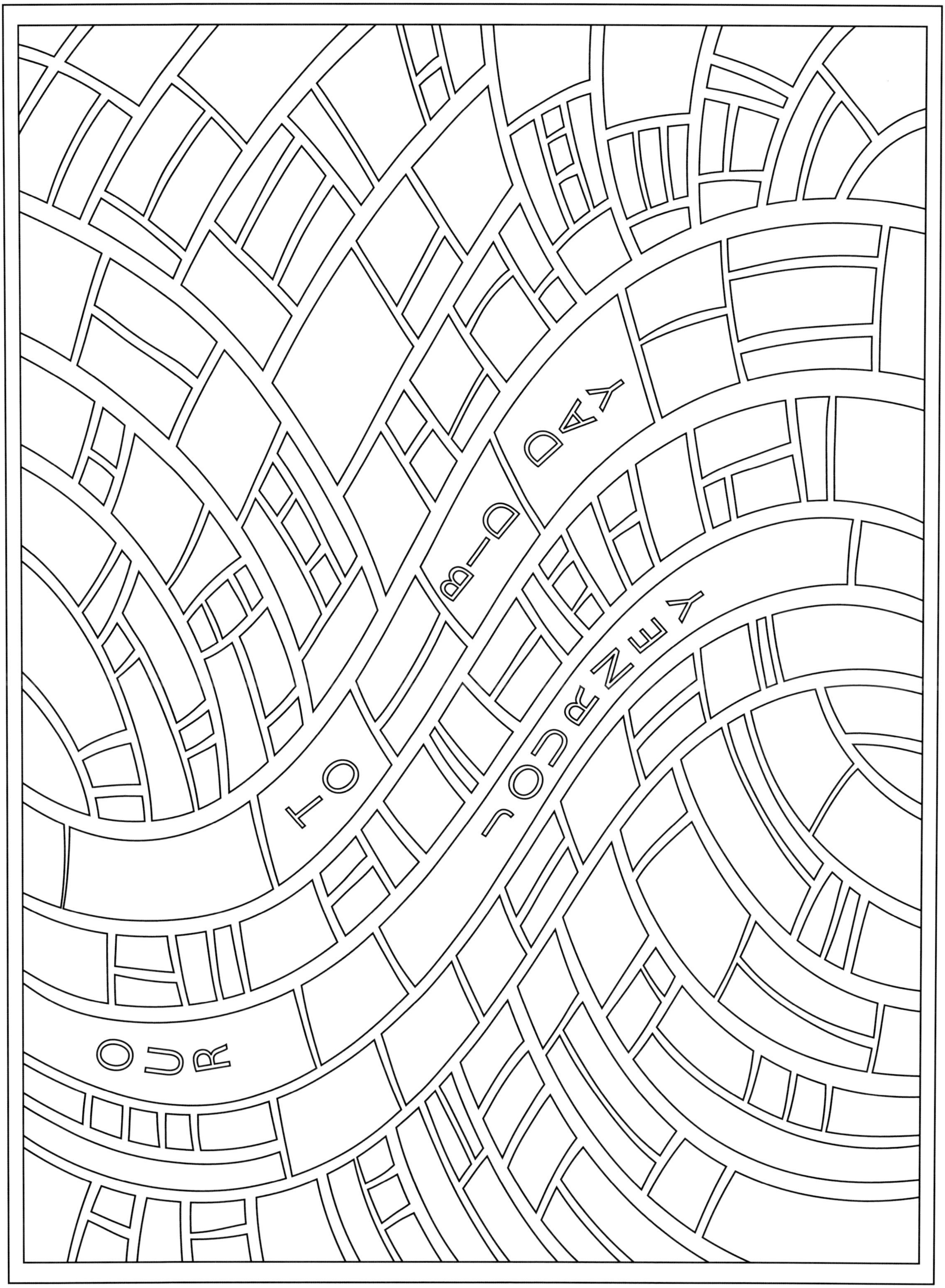
OUR
JOURNEY
TO
B-D
DAY

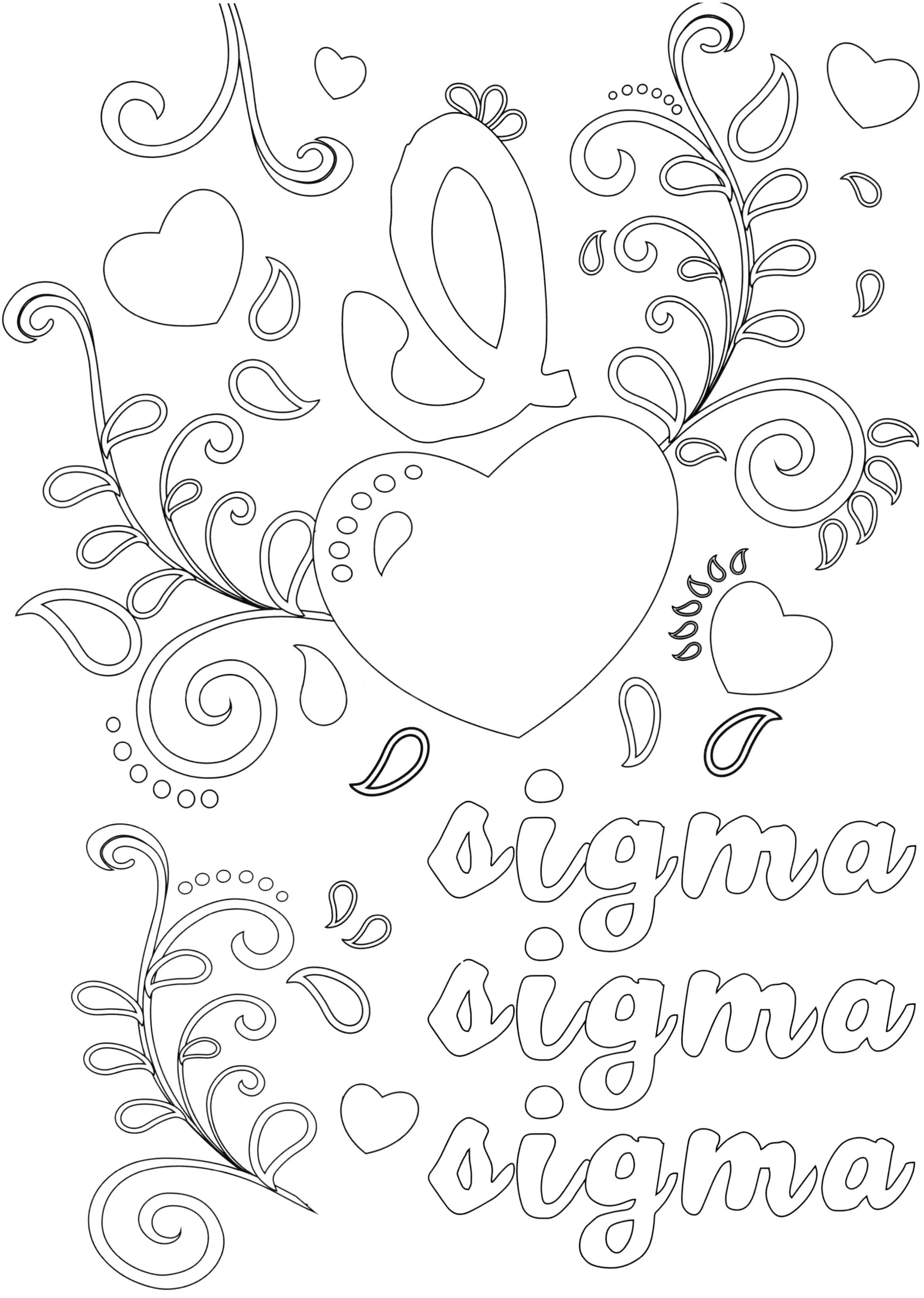
I
sigma
sigma
sigma

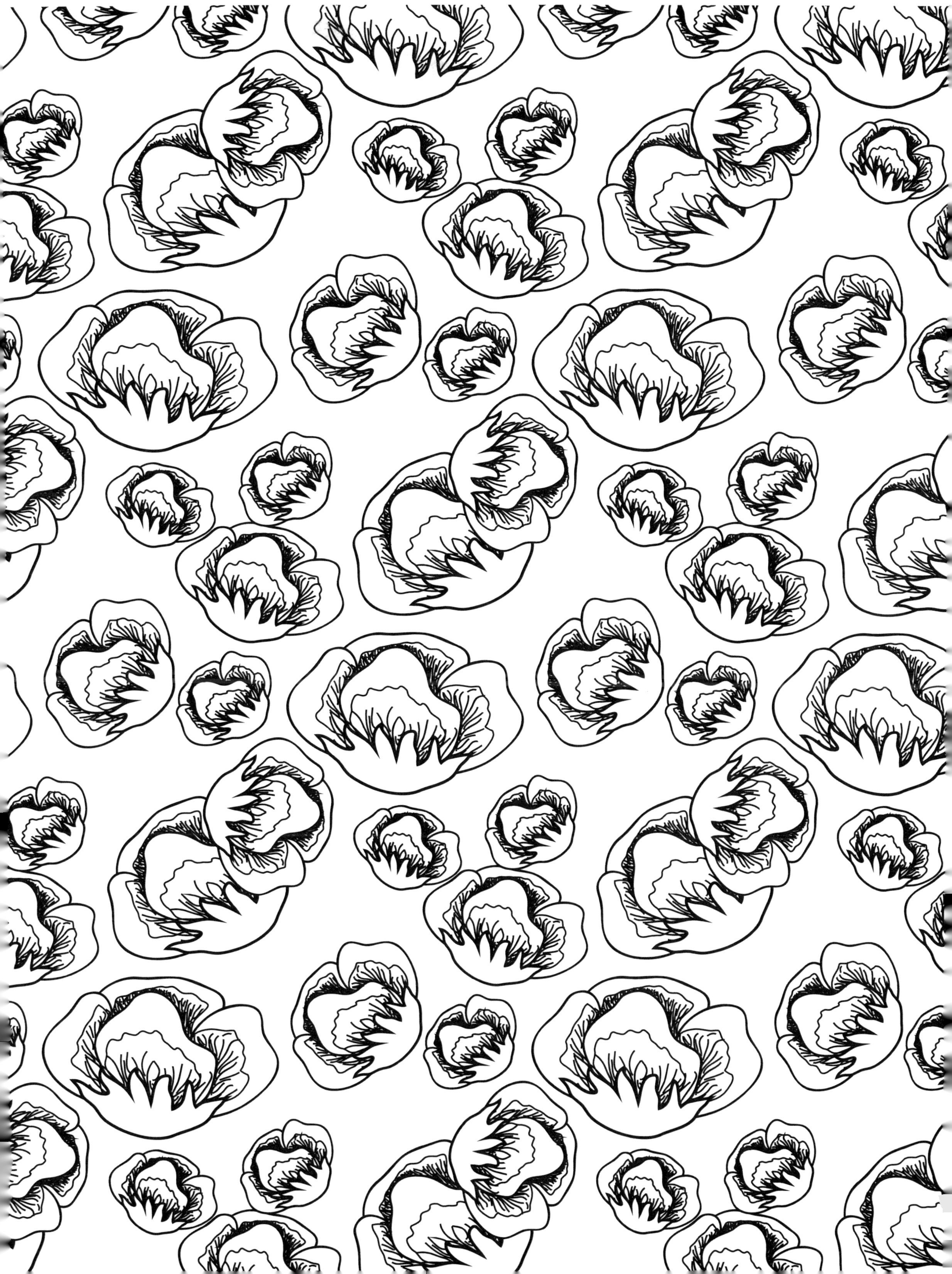

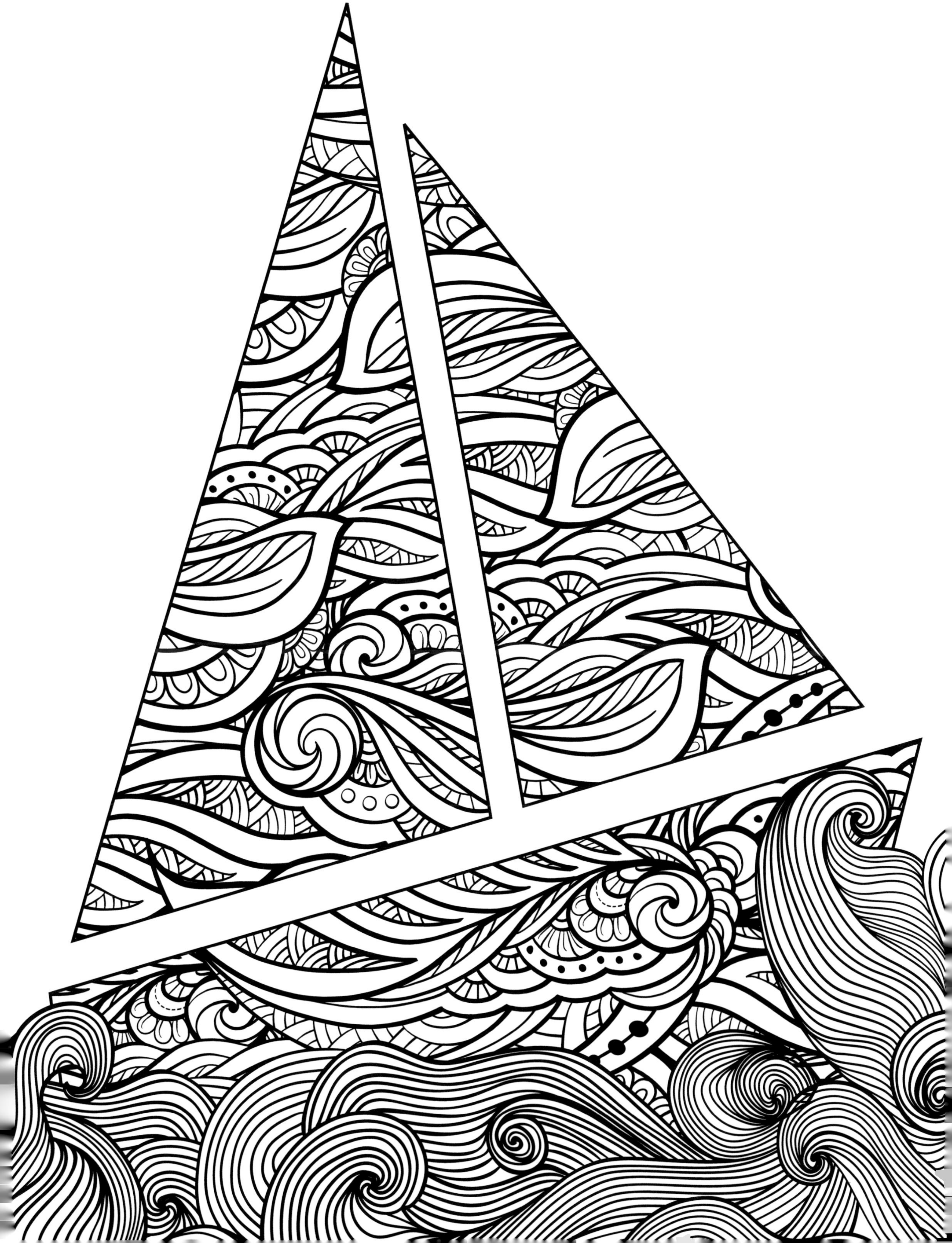

ΣΣΣ

These letters
don't make me
better
than you,
they make me
better than who
I used to be

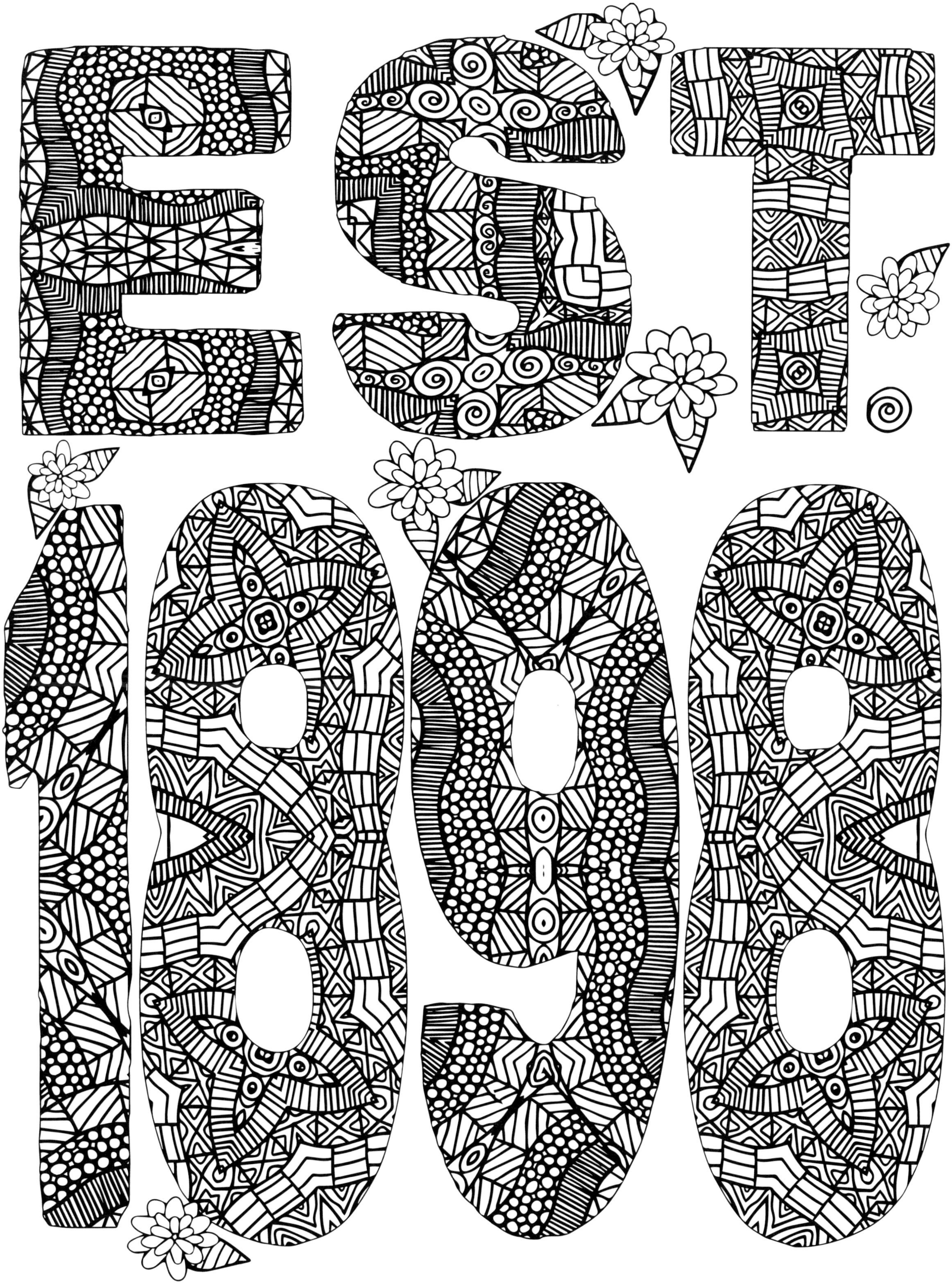
EST.
1998

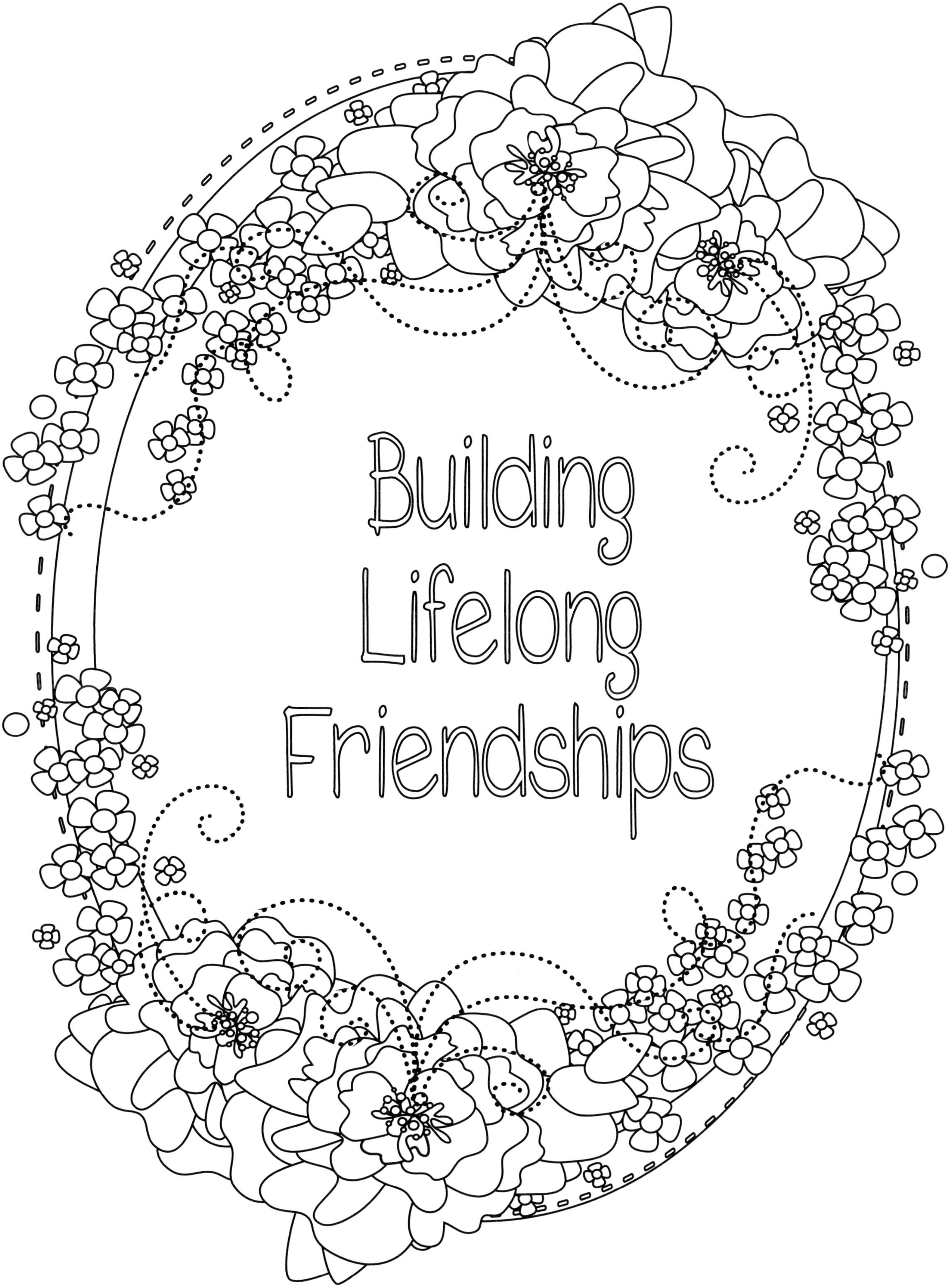
Building
Lifelong
Friendships

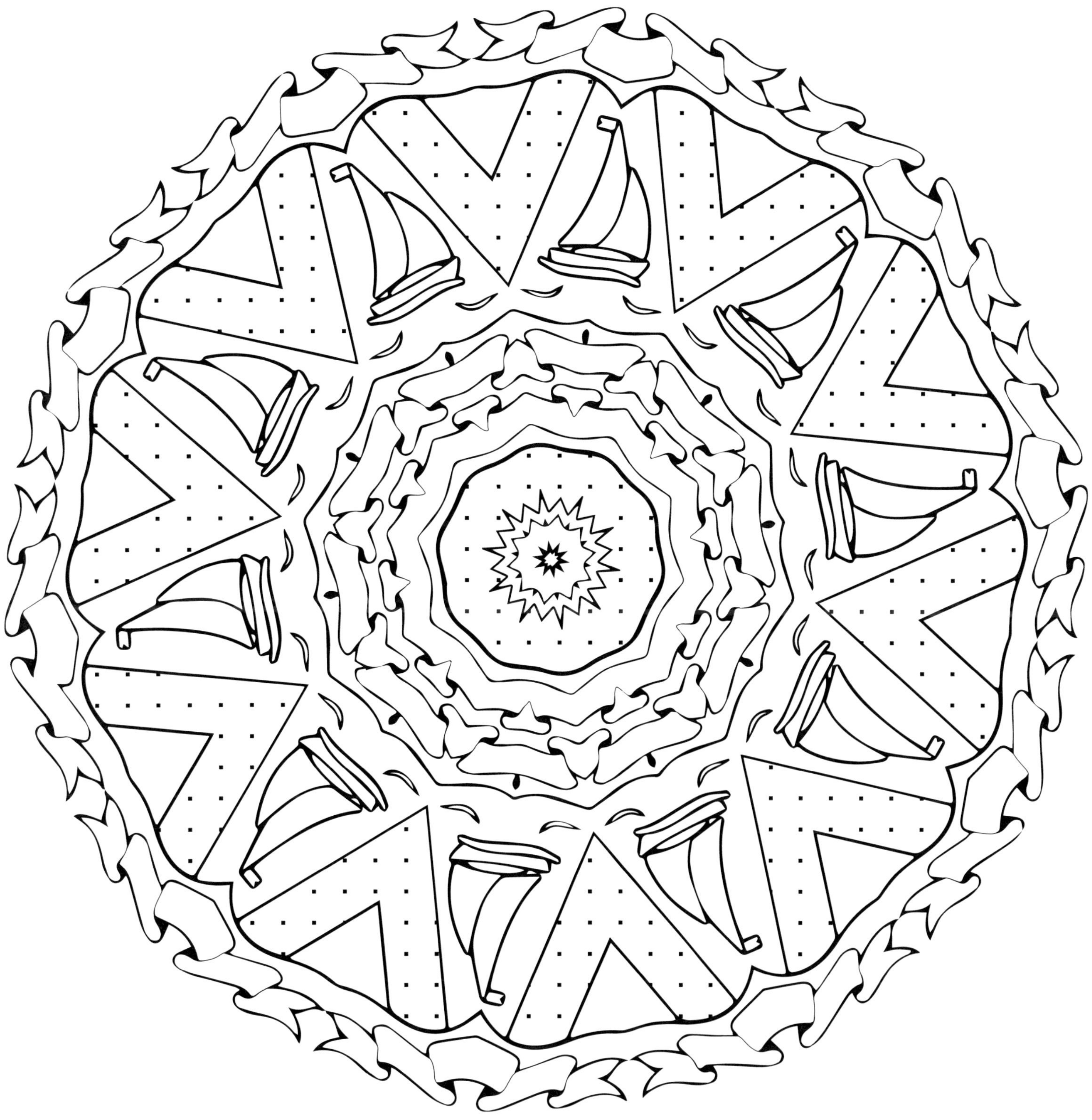

Leadership

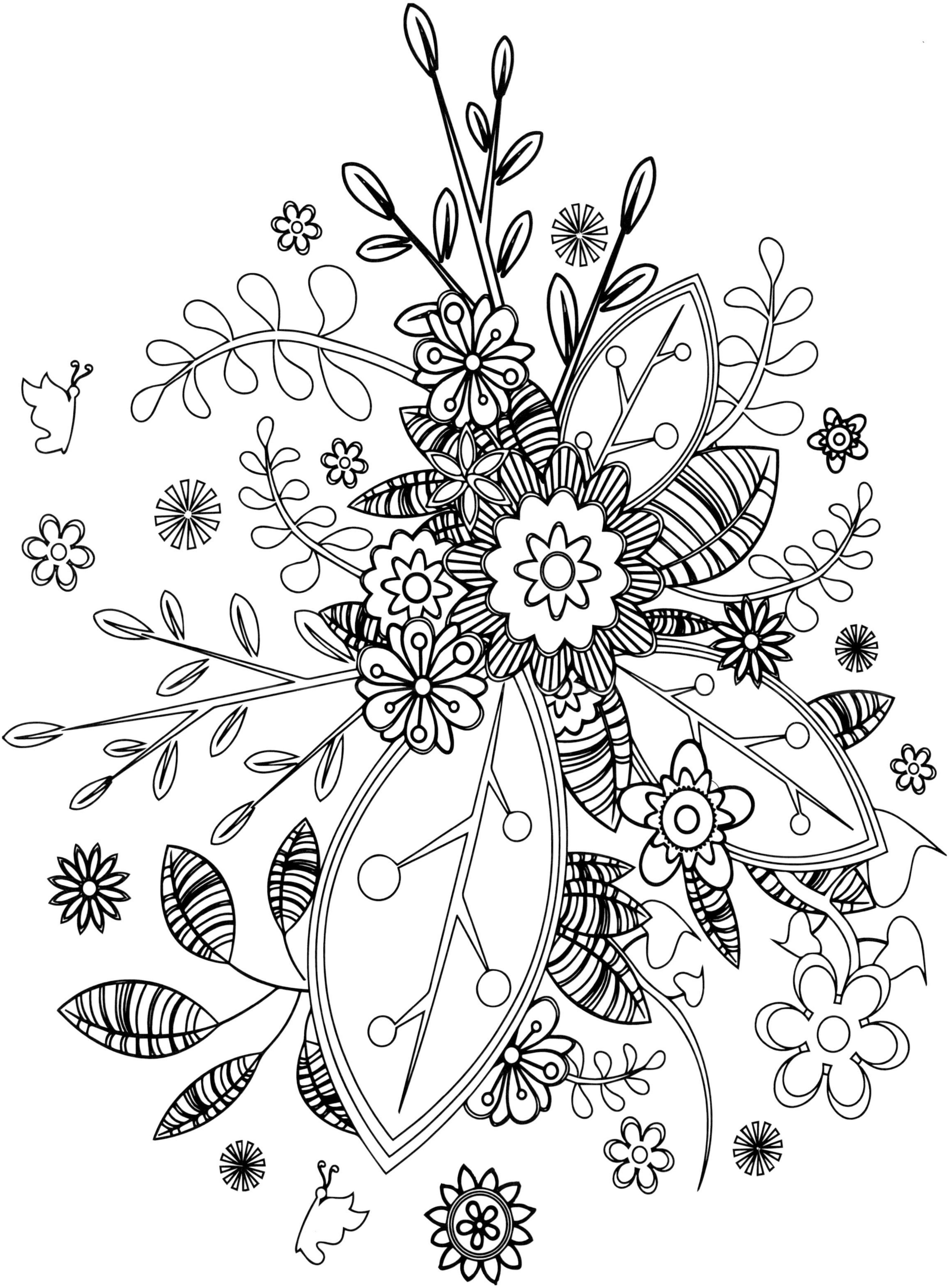

Here's to you
Here's to me

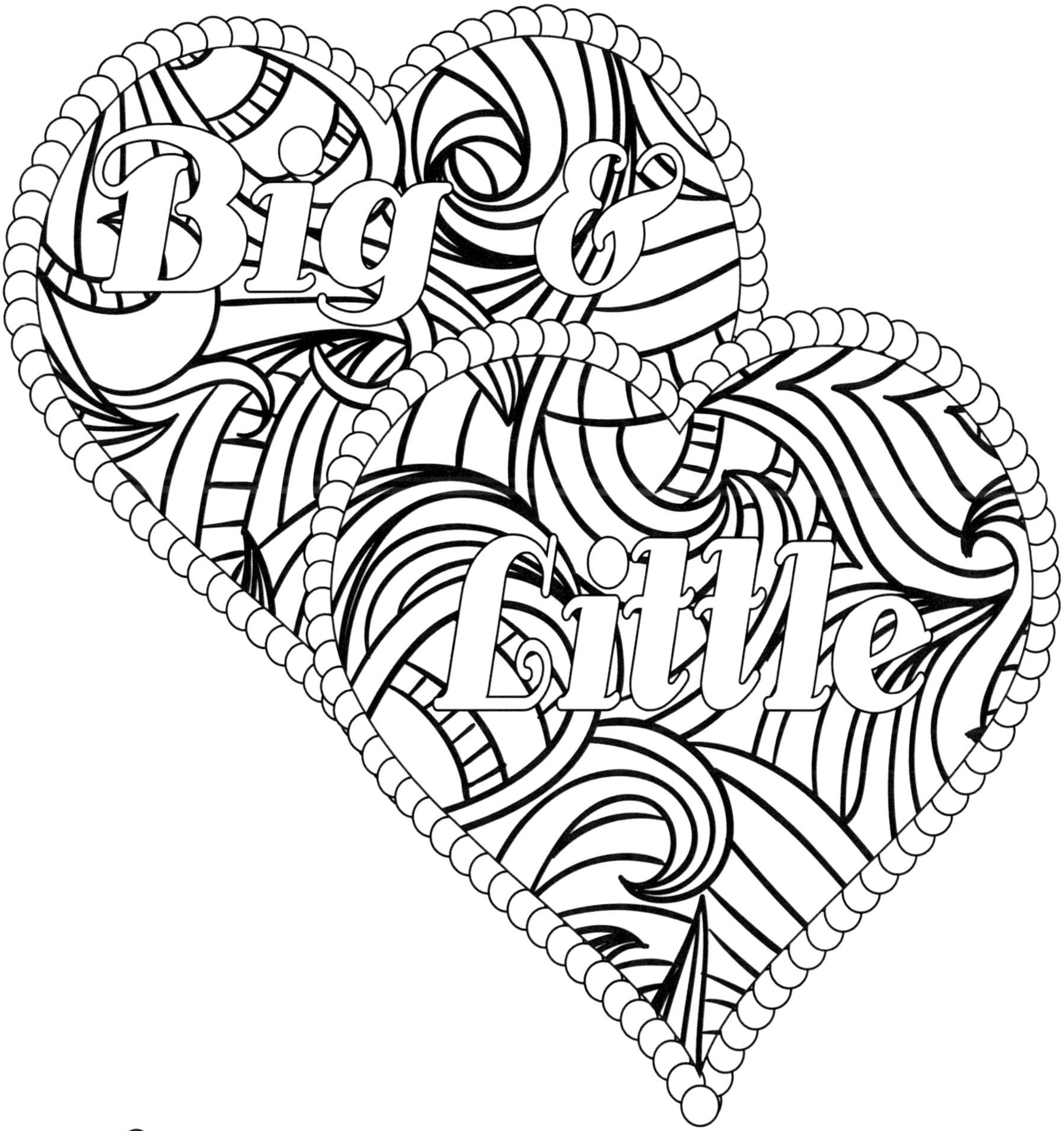

We'll always be

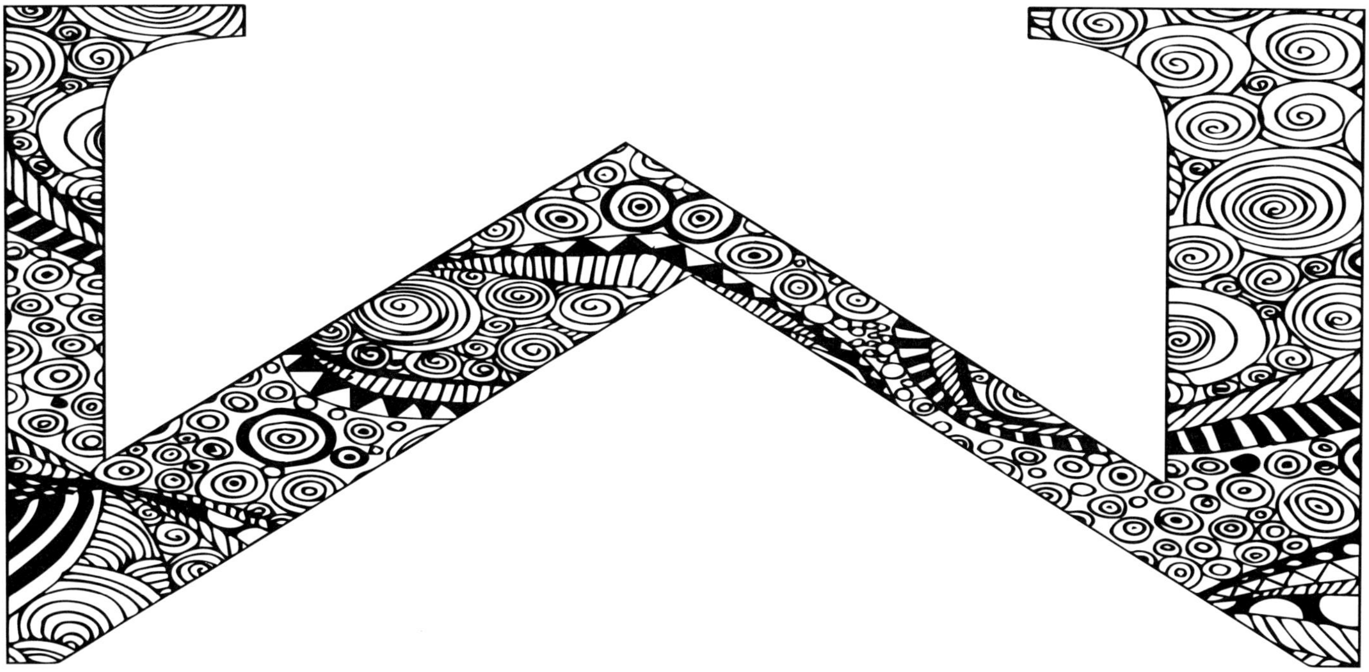
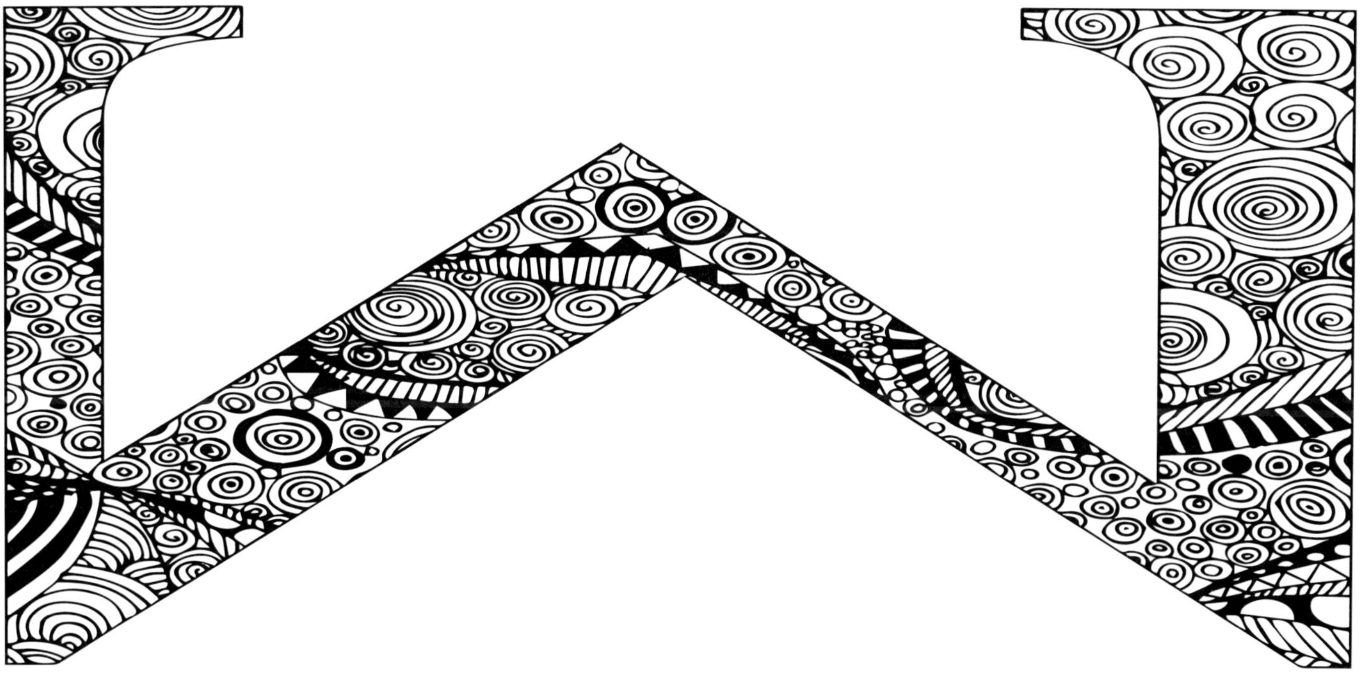
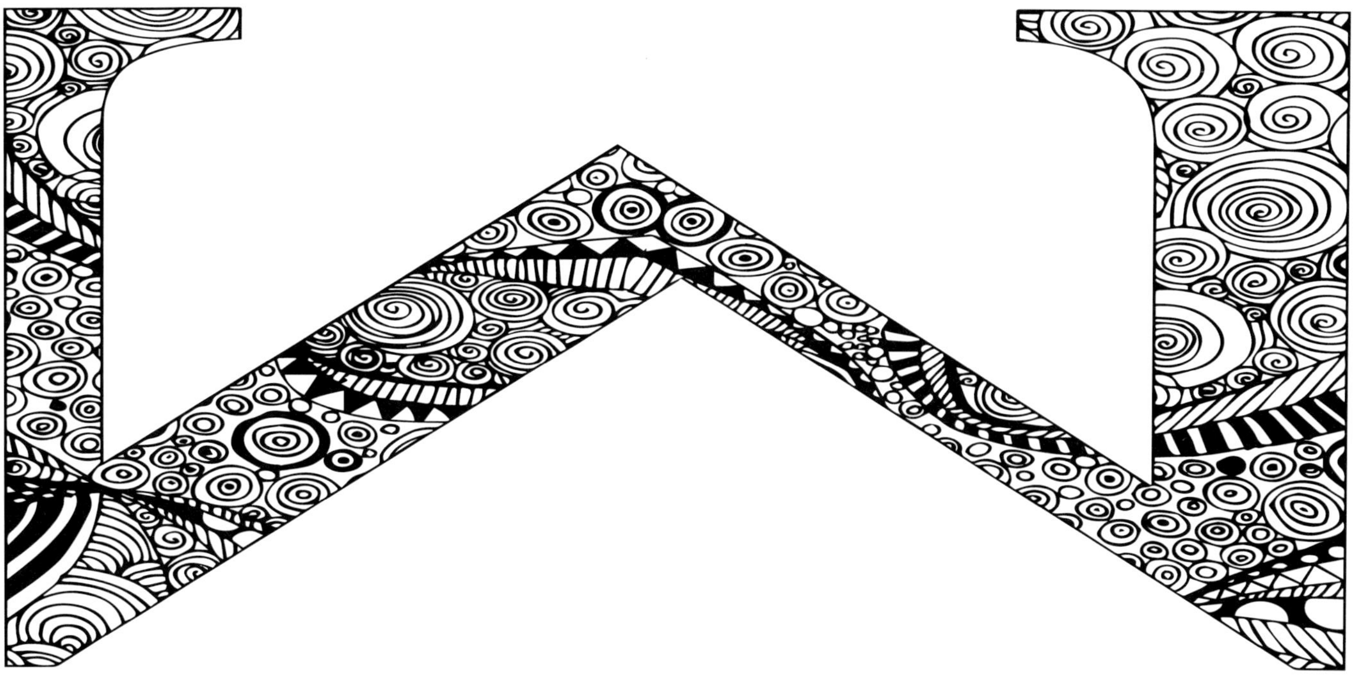

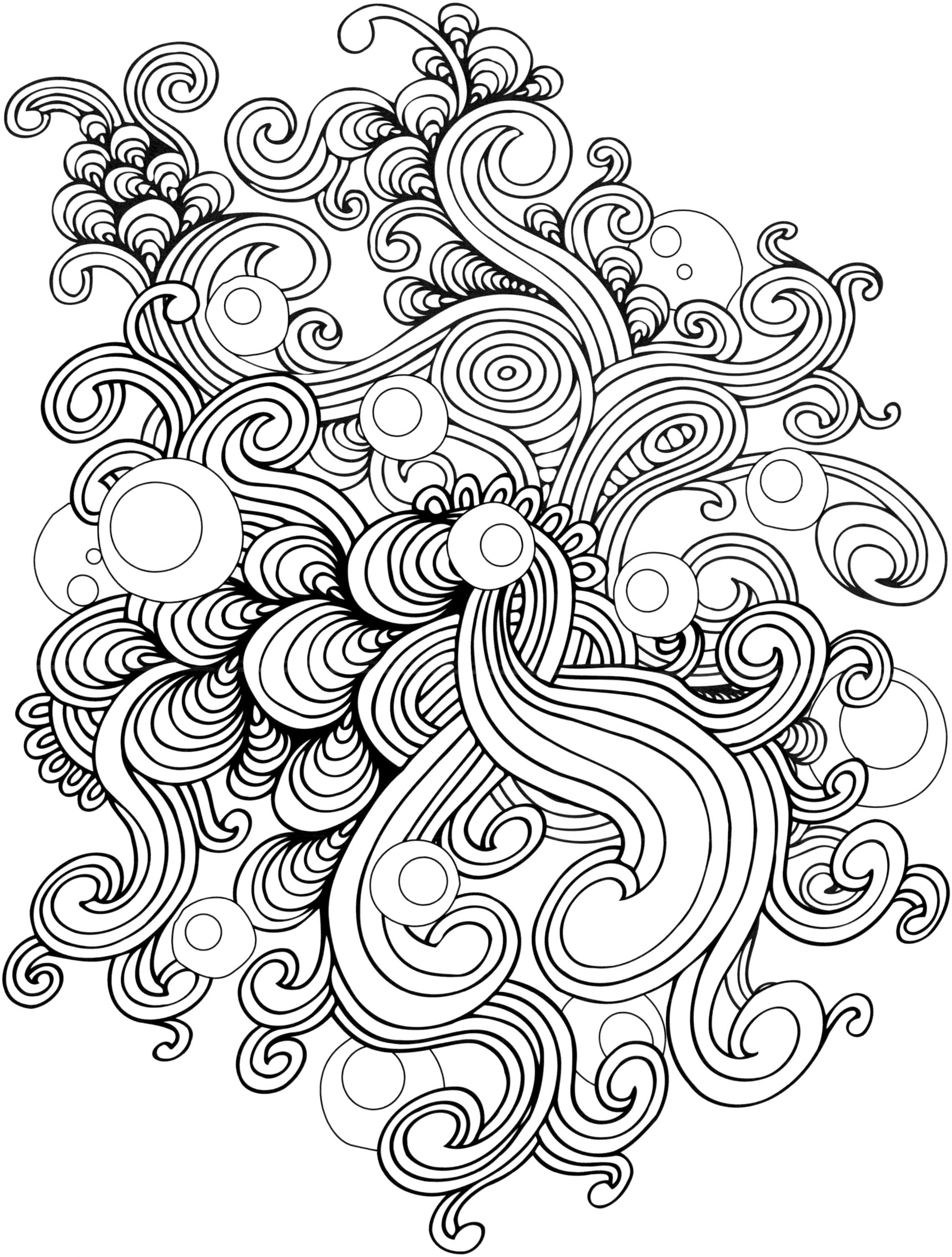

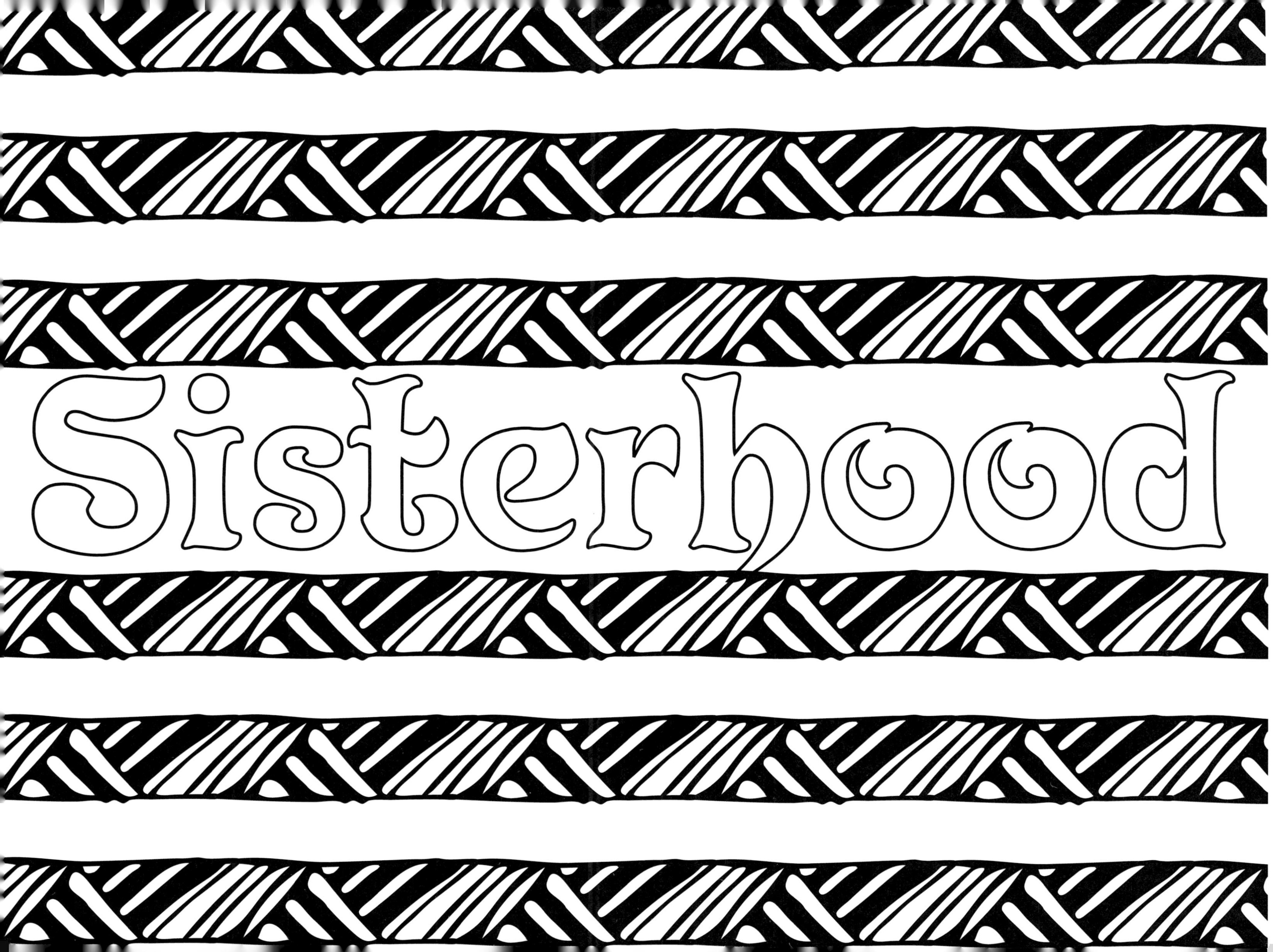
Sisterhood

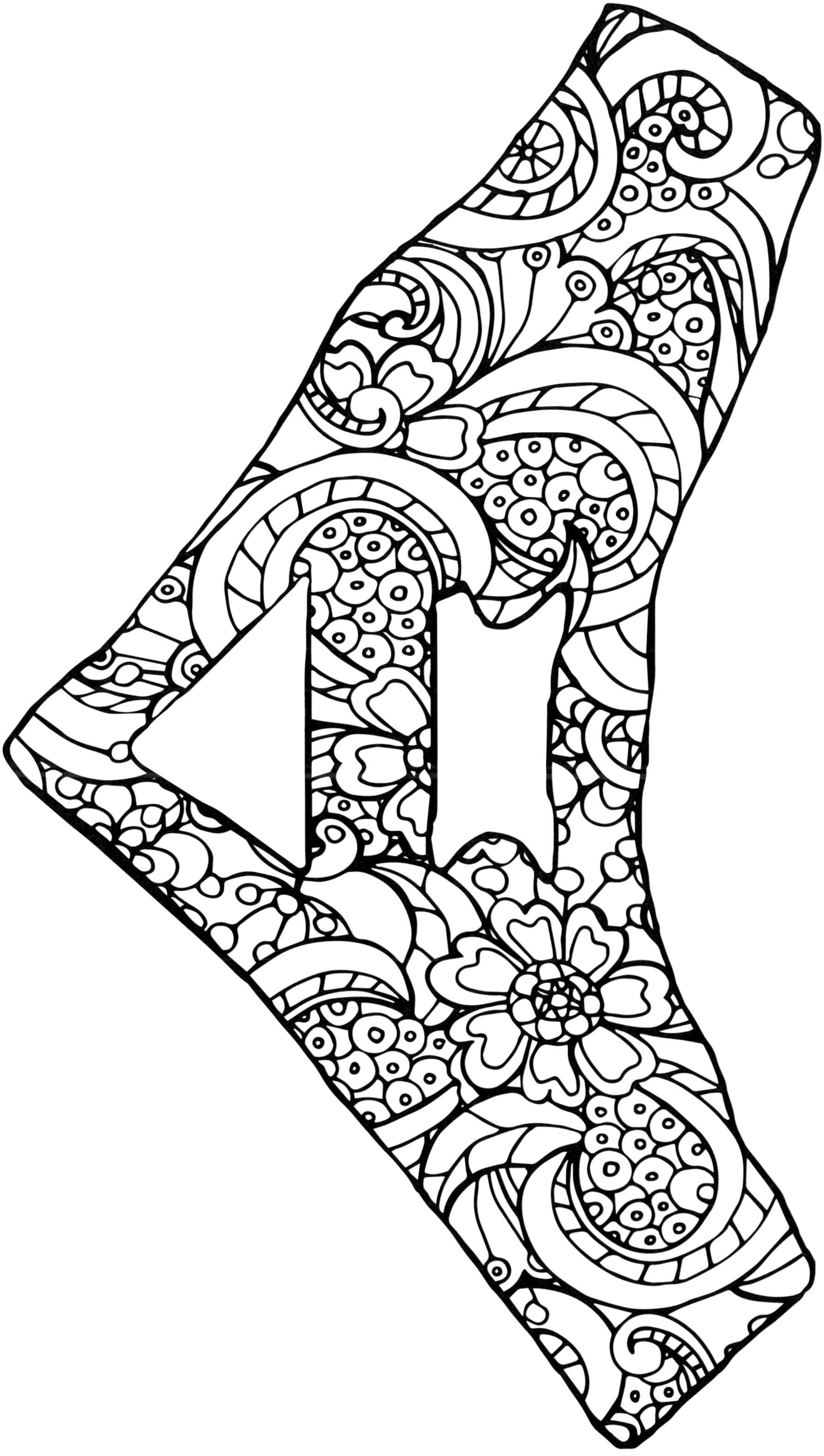

Ever forward

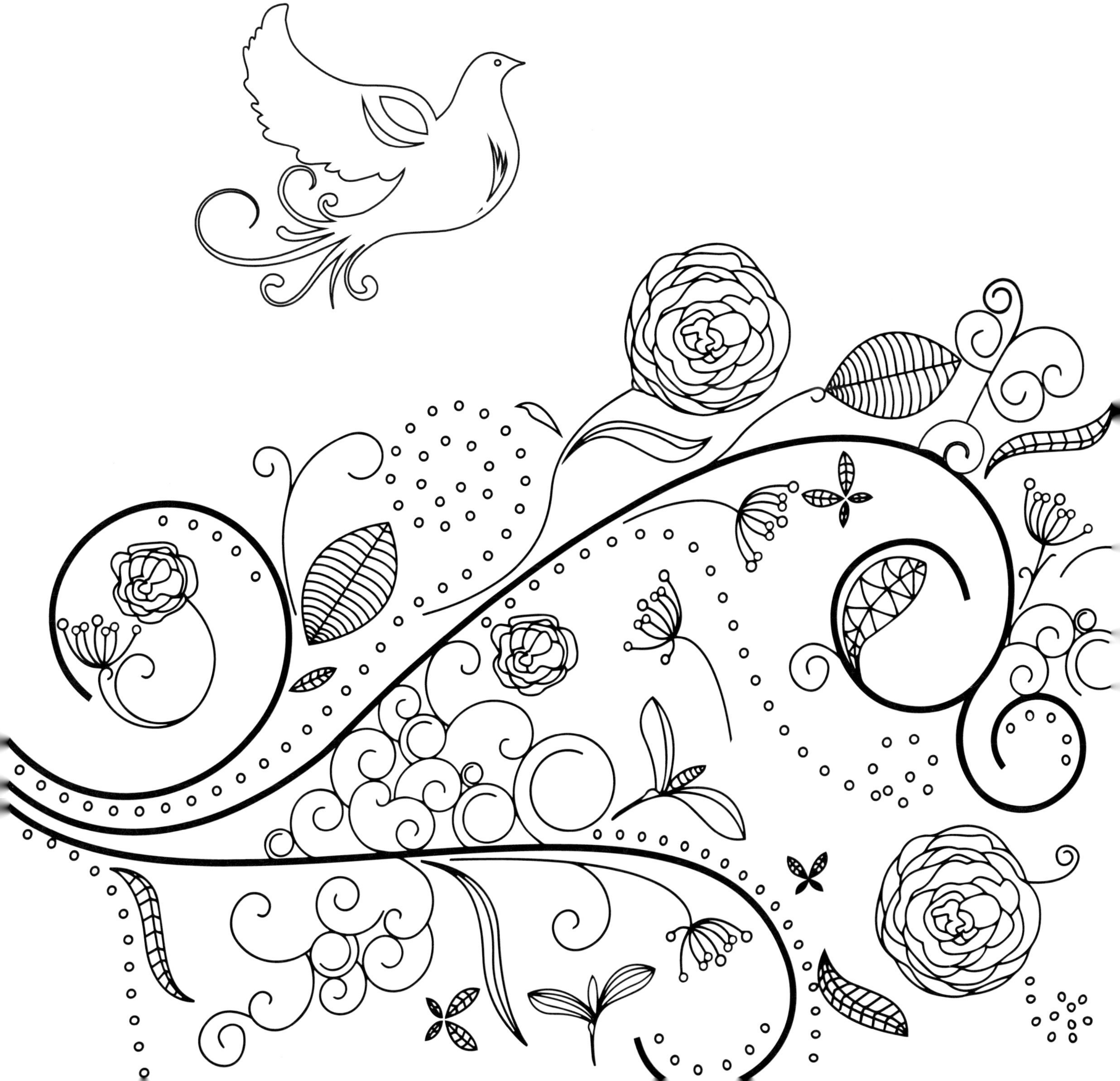

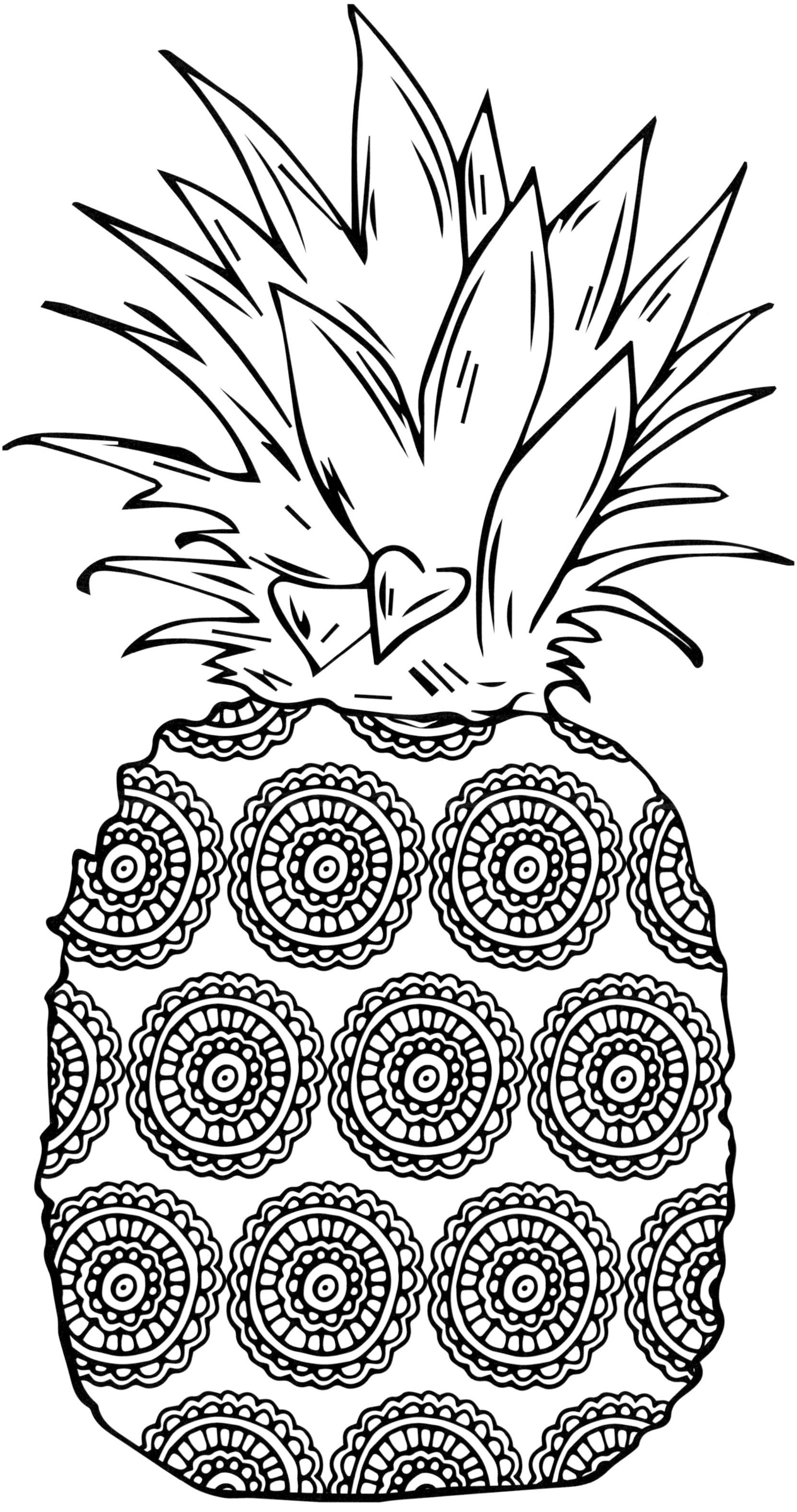

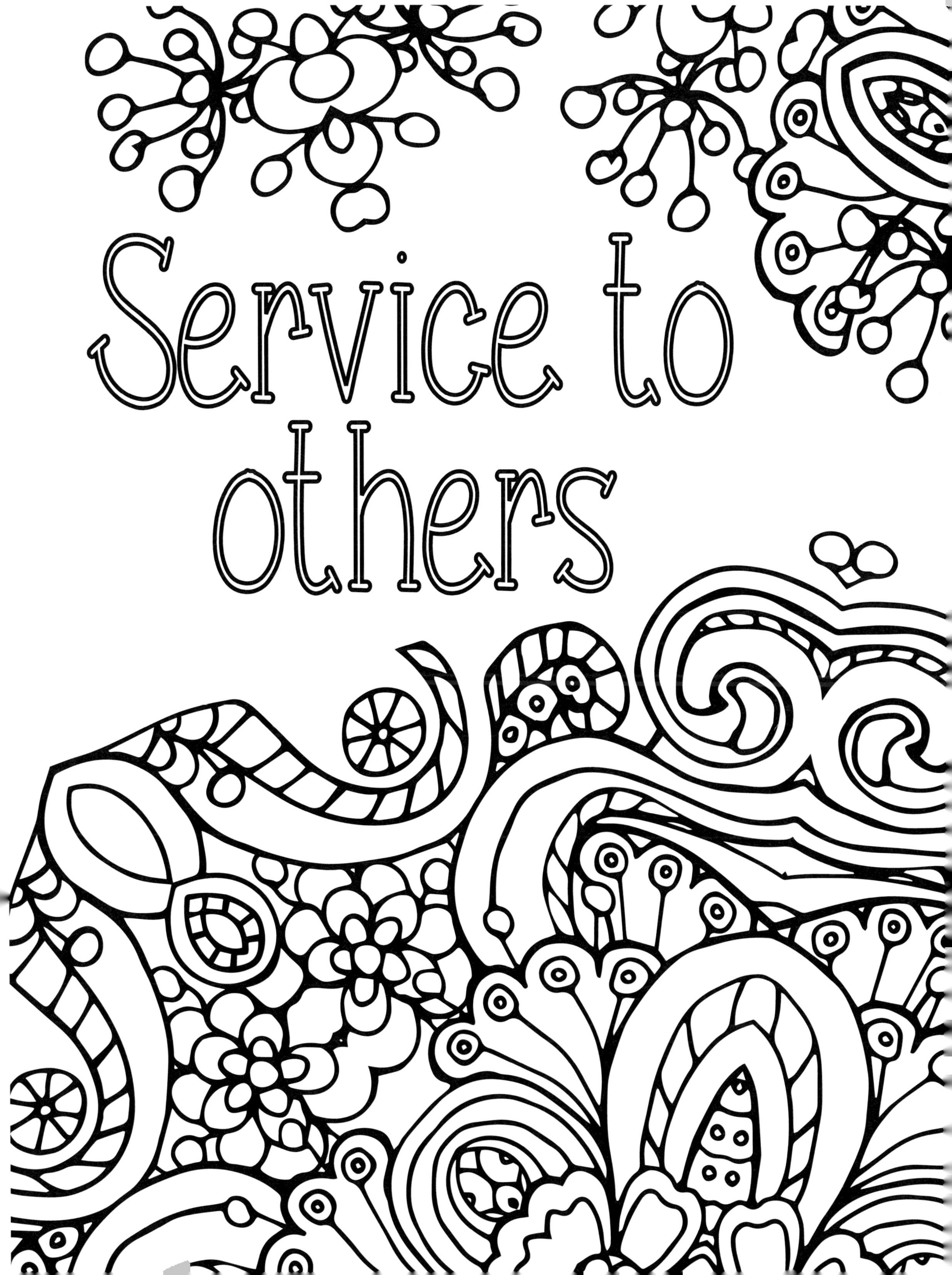
Service to others